KOKOPELLI

Lawrence W. Cheek

LOOK WEST
SERIES

RIO NUEVO PUBLISHERS
TUCSON, ARIZONA

On a basalt escarpment in the high desert of
northern New Mexico, a prehistoric procession of five
hunchbacked flute players dances across a rock.
It is an orchestra frozen in time, and modern wanderers
who stumble across it may feel more than one shiver
navigating through their spines. First comes the delight of
recognition: the flute player parades across hundreds of
petroglyph sites scattered across the American southwest.
But at this unusual site, another feeling
also arises backstage in the mind, something
faintly unsettling, even eerie.

The ancient flute player most commonly appears as a soloist, a single figure in an apparent clutter of humans, animals, and abstract figures scratched and pecked into rock. But this panel has the air of a sacred ceremony, perhaps one inaccessible to ordinary mortals. It

Near Santa Fe, a prehistoric orchestra dances across an escarpment.

may be a landscape of spirits—but who or what are they? What does the ceremony mean, and why was it recorded on this particular stone, perhaps uniquely? Was the flute player something more than the cheerful fertility figure or good-luck charm that we so casually assume today?

"Casual" isn't quite the right word. The figure we commonly call "Kokopelli" re-emerged in the late twentieth century as a modern icon of the American Southwest and more. One hardly has to prowl the canyons of New Mexico, Utah, or Arizona to stumble onto him today. Kokopelli cookie cutters stamp out gingerbread flutists, and tattoo artists adorn arms and legs with contemporary variations on the prehistoric image. A Google search heaves up 206,000 hits, hundreds of them commercial enterprises, which literally span the globe. Kokopelli Native American Cedar Flutes. Kokopelli Rafting Adventures. Kokopelli's Cave Bed &

Contemporary paintings of the Ancient Ones by Navajo artist Nathaniel Gorman of Chinle, Arizona.

Breakfast. Kokopelli Winery. A Kokopelli Golf Course in Arizona and another in Illinois. KoKoPelli's Mexican Grill (offering franchises—hurry!). Kokopelli Arts Webdesign. A Kokopelli Choir based in Edmonton, Alberta. *Les Semances de Kokopelli,* a French association promoting the biodiversity of seeds. *Kokopelli.de—Magazin für Kunst und Kultur,* a German online magazine of art and culture. And Kokopelli.com, a Texas-based department store offering Kokopelli clocks, socks, garden stepping-stones, refrigerator magnets, and spoon rests.

There has never been anything quite like this contemporary Kokopelli craze—except the Kokopelli phenomenon of a millennium past. The prehistoric flutist's wanderings and possible iconic meanings were incredibly fluid. He danced across cultural and linguistic boundaries with apparent ease, appeared in countless bodily forms and symbolic roles, and persisted for about eight hundred years, wandering at least once as far north as the Canadian Rocky Mountains of Alberta, east to the Oklahoma panhandle,

and into Mexico to the present-day Sonoran town of Caborca. Whatever the figure's meaning, it wasn't "casual" in prehistoric times, either.

KOKOPELLI'S BIRTH AND LIFE

The now-familiar flute player probably first appeared in petroglyph form in the Four Corners area of the American Southwest during Basketmaker III times, A.D. 500–750. "Probably" is an irritating but necessary qualifier, because rock art is notoriously difficult to date. Using dendrochronology (tree-ring dating), archaeologists can often nail the exact years of a prehistoric pueblo's construction and abandonment, but rock art in the same neighborhood doesn't necessarily correspond—it might have been the work of people who lived there or of those who simply passed by at another time. Archaeologists make their best guesses based on artifacts they find in the nearest dig and on the subject or style of the rock art. Sometimes petroglyphs from different eras will be scratched onto the same rock, and the relative weathering of the patina—the iron and manganese oxide stain on the rock surface—will roughly suggest the span of time between the etchings.

This figure plays an unusually long and curved instrument (near Holbrook, Arizona).

By A.D. 1000, Kokopelli figures were migrating through the river valleys of northeastern Arizona, northwestern New Mexico, and eastern Utah. Most of this is Anasazi territory, but images of the flute player also turned up in northern Utah's Fremont culture, southern New Mexico's Mogollon, and central Arizona's Hohokam. Guest appearances on the Great Plains, in the Canadian Rockies, and in Mexico remained rare. Intriguingly, although the Hohokam rarely etched the flute player's image into rock, they liberally painted him on their ceramic wares—as did the Anasazi.

In the late 1200s the Anasazi culture flew apart in a cataclysmic time of drought, environmental exhaustion, and warfare that archaeologists call "the abandonment." Many of the survivors trickled over to the Rio Grande Valley, where their Pueblo descendants live today. Others migrated to the Hopi mesas of Arizona. Eventually new Kokopelli appearances grew rarer and, after the Spanish *entrada* into the Southwest in the 1500s, ceased entirely.

The term "Anasazi" means "ancient enemies" in the Navajo language. Modern Pueblo people, who are descended from these cliff-dwelling people, prefer the term "Ancestral Puebloans."

Rainfall averages less than nine inches a year at Petrified Forest National Park, but
Puebloan farmers still worked the land—and these rocks.

The original Kokopelli was a simple stick or outline human figure playing a flute—nothing more. (Native American flutes, made of bone or wood, were held and blown straight away from the mouth like the baroque recorder, rather than held transversely like the modern orchestral flute. Kokopelli petroglyphs and paintings are always in profile, since this is the only way to illustrate the flute.) As the centuries passed, the musician seemed to acquire personality—or more accurately, multiple personalities. Usually he seemed jaunty, but he could also appear comical, dignified, purposeful, or ghostly. He also took on quite a variety of appendages: a backpack or hunchback, obtrusive and sometimes webbed feet, and a dramatic headdress that could have been fashioned of feathers—although occasionally it more resembled insect antennae. In fact, Kokopelli sometimes appeared to *be* an insect. Possible connections include a Zuni legend about a flute-playing cicada and a hunchbacked Hopi katsina based on the robber fly (though the latter doesn't carry an instrument). We can find a few Kokopelli figures bearing the head of a bird and a few wearing a tail. On rare occasions, he holds a cane or a bow instead of a flute. The figures appear in every imaginable pose: standing upright, walking, dancing, sitting, kneeling, reclining, and—copulating.

A rudimentary hunchback appears on this stick-figure flutist (south-central New Mexico).

Which brings us to the most obvious and intriguing feature of all: the phallus, erect and often prominently exaggerated. The Anasazi Kokopelli acquired a phallus and hunchback sometime after the basic Basketmaker renderings, and at his prime—probably A.D. 1000–1400—almost always was portrayed with both. Sometimes the phallic Kokopelli appears in proximity to a female figure, where the implication is obvious. In other panels, he floats among assorted animals, sun and cloud motifs, and (to us) abstract figures. The New Mexico procession of five phallic Kokopellis appears to dance in an arc toward a natural feature in the rock that could be interpreted as female—or are our overactive imaginations operating here? Intriguingly, the Hohokam flute player appears on prehistoric pots and bowls without phallus, as he does in modern renderings on all those sweatshirts and spoon rests—neutered and G-rated.

ABOVE: In Hohokam culture, the flutist appeared on ceramics such as this Red-on-buff plate (from the Snaketown site, south of Phoenix). RIGHT: A recumbent flute player (top right) inhabits this Anasazi panel (Little Colorado River area, Arizona).

The curved back has been interpreted from time to time as a trader's backpack, a quiver for arrows, a piggyback rider, and a physical deformity. A deformity seems most likely. In prehistoric Mesoamerica (central Mexico south to present-day Nicaragua), supernatural powers were ascribed to hunchbacks; they were rendered in architecture, sculpture, and ceramics as persons of apparent high status. Anthropologist Joyce Alpert has developed perhaps the most intriguing theory about Kokopelli, linking the hunchback and erect phallus with an actual medical condition called Pott's disease, or tuberculosis of the spine.

Pott's disease causes vertebrae to collapse, deforming the spine into a curve that might, in some cases, resemble a hump. In males, the unusual pressure on the spinal cord can cause another

Contemporary Navajo weaving (Visitors Center, Monument Valley Tribal Park, Utah).

symptom called priapism, a permanent, non-sexual erection. It also can cause foot deformities, such as clubfoot—and some depictions of Kokopelli indeed depict one foot as misshapen or swollen. Physical anthropologists have examined abnormal human skeletons from prehistoric sites in both North and South America, including some in the American Southwest, and have concluded that spinal tuberculosis was the likely cause of such abnormalities. There is little doubt, Alpert concluded, that the petroglyph portraits reflect the symptoms of a human with Pott's disease "appropriately and explicitly."

BUT WHAT DOES HE MEAN?

Interpreting rock art is one of modern archaeology's most slippery slopes. Does it form narratives, such as a creation story or the record of a clan's migrations? Ceremonial offerings or, in a sense, engraved prayers? Territorial markers? Symbolic communications intended to convey esoteric knowledge to future generations?

Probably rock art served all these functions. The one quality archaeologists all agree on: it was not trivial, certainly nothing like the modern graffiti that, sadly, has defaced some prehistoric sites. Pecking a petroglyph into rock using another rock as a tool is hard

work; the creators clearly meant the images to be permanent. Otherwise, why not just carve them on tree bark?

But what information do the images convey? Modern Native Americans sometimes can provide clues. A retired Southwest book editor I know tells a story about showing a photograph of a petroglyph, perhaps a thousand years old, to a Hopi friend, who exclaimed delightedly, "That's my name!" Scratched into the rock was a cross-hatched rectangle rising vertically out of a field of wavy parallel lines. The Hopi read it as "corn-standing-in-water," which was indeed the friend's name. Unfortunately, most examples are not so obvious or clear. Modern native people frequently disagree on the interpretation of a particular image.

Polly Schaafsma, the anthropologist who wrote the definitive book on Southwestern rock art in 1980, says that rock art buffs tend to see what they are already predisposed to. The figures, she says, provide "a kind of Rorschach test in which the observer projects onto the drawings meanings that coincide with cultural biases and personal and popular fantasies."

Kokopelli presents a particularly knotty case. Modern purveyors of Kokopelliana have endowed the figure with a dazzling array of

Two flute players at Sand Island Recreational Area (near Bluff, Utah).

identities and powers: mischievous trickster, rainmaker, storyteller, fertility god, even the "Anasazi Casanova." "He represents abundance and prosperity," says the owner of a Kokopelli bed and breakfast. "Legend has it," another commercial purveyor maintains, "everyone in the village would sing and dance throughout the night when they heard Kokopelli play his flute. The next morning, every maiden in the village would be with child."

Much of this is modern fantasy; some of it might have roots in Pueblo mythology. Assorted Hopi sources, speaking to archaeologists, have identified Kokopelli as a clan symbol—although *which* clan seems to be in some doubt. The Flute Clan, Spider Clan, Water Clan, and Titmouse Clan have all been suggested.

In a remarkable book published in 2000 titled *Kokopelli: The Making of an Icon,* Northern Arizona University linguist Ekkehart Malotki sleuthed back through the Hopi language—his specialty— and religion to debunk the associations that the modern world has ascribed to the ancient flutist. "The current popularity of Kokopelli is based on a misunderstanding," Malotki insists.

Pioneer Southwestern archaeologist Jesse Walter Fewkes was the first to christen the flute-playing petroglyph "Kokopeli" (his spelling)

A lavish Anasazi panel, apparently looted with a chisel (near Holbrook, Arizona).

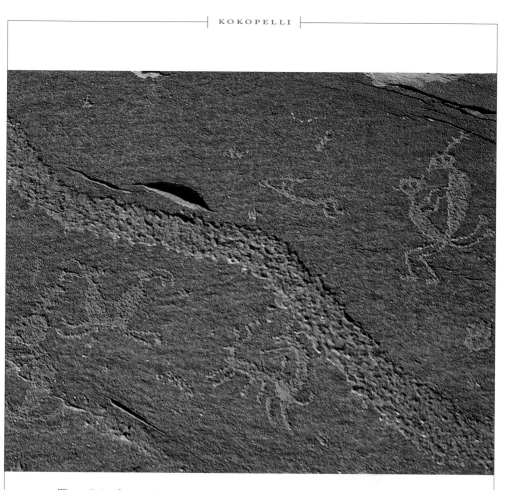

The reclining figure in this north central Arizona panel appears to be serenading amorous couples, perhaps supporting the link between fertility and the flute player.

in 1898. Fewkes and the authorities who followed him apparently picked up this notion from the name of the Hopi katsina Kookopölö, a benevolent spirit associated with the rains that deliver good crops and also with human fertility.

The link to the petroglyph seemed reasonable, because the personification of Kookopölö in masked dancers and dolls featured a hunchback, a headdress, and, before modern sensibilities edited his anatomy, a prominent phallus. And the direct line from Pueblo culture to Hopi culture has never been in question.

But as Malotki points out, there was one glaring inconsistency in the conclusion: the katsina Kookopölö never played a flute. The katsina did bear an extended nose, however, so anthropologists assumed that the instrument had morphed into something new—a "nose whistle," one account suggested.

Kookopölö (hunchbacked or Robber Fly katsina) by Hopi artist Cecil Calnimptewa.

In Hopi theology and ceremony, Kookopölö is a vivid and potent fertility figure, "jumping up and down among the women" and impregnating those who have tried and thus far failed to conceive. His female counterpart, Kokopölmana, is also overtly sex-crazed, appearing to lure and chase men and simulate copulation with her "victims." Malotki traces the katsina's origins back to an insect—the robber fly, which Hopis observed to be a prodigious copulator. But as a katsina, Kookopölö is more than a lecherous playboy. He also happens to be an industrious and successful farmer, which is why the women readily gravitate toward him. Thus not only is reproduction assured, but also prosperity.

Kokopölmana (hunchbacked or Robber Fly katsina maiden)
by Hopi artist Brian Honyouti.

This faded flute player was painted on volcanic rock near Flagstaff, Arizona—Sinagua territory.

So is there any linkage—aside from certain anatomical features—between the Kokopelli scratched into rock and the Kookopölö etched into the Hopi pantheon? Malotki thinks not. Anthropologist and writer Scott Thybony also reports a telling encounter with Ebin Leslie, head priest of the Hopi Blue Flute Clan:

He wore his graying hair tied in a knot and a heavy silver ring depicting a man bent over, playing a flute. I made the mistake of calling it a Kokopelli. The figure on the ring is not Kokopelli but a flute player, Lahlanhoya, Delfred [Leslie's son] said as he translated … Though often confused, they are not the same entity … Delfred said the flute player, Lahlanhoya, is a clan symbol. On their migrations, the Flute Clan left the emblem carved and painted on cliffs and village walls throughout the Southwest. Every detail of the flute player has meaning, and surrounding figures can be important. Horned animals are often found with the flute player. Bighorns are trailblazers, always taking the lead. They scout the way ahead and find water. They were the ones to locate the trail the Flute Clan took to reach First Mesa.

A flute player serenades an anthropomorphic figure with exaggerated hands and feet and ceremonial plumage (San Juan River area, Utah).

That might seem to resolve the question except for a few nagging details: How did this one of many Puebloan clan symbols also happen to have a prominent role in Hohokam ceramics and wander up to the Rockies of Canada and the Sonoran Desert of Mexico? Why did the flute player's appearance and position and apparent mood vary so widely and change so radically over his very long lifetime?

Dennis Slifer and James Duffield, two New Mexico geologists who have meticulously surveyed Kokopelli rock-art portraits throughout the Southwest, offer this suggestion: "The great number and variety of prehistoric figures identified as Kokopelli are probably related through a continuum of mythic beings that has evolved and diffused throughout the Southwest over time." All human cultures adopt myths from their forebears or neighbors, adapting them to current social and religious needs. Kokopelli clearly served more than one culture and probably more than one purpose.

And what about the genesis of the myth? Joyce Alpert serves up a tantalizing theory: that the flute player *wasn't* a myth, but an actual human being afflicted with Pott's disease. "For an individual bearing such disabilities to be acceptable to Puebloan culture, a culture that traditionally rejected unusual-appearing individuals,

Anasazi flute player, far right (San Juan Basin, New Mexico).

he would have had to bring special attributes that would benefit that group," she writes. "The Puebloan people, dependent upon agricultural fertility, might revere a culture hero that, with his priapism, appeared to represent fertility."

It's an intriguing theory, but there's also a problem with it: Pott's disease is painful, and any jarring or twisting of the spine causes distress. People who have the disease don't dance or even walk normally; they shuffle as if gliding over ice, to avoid even minor impacts to the deformed spine. How to explain Kokopelli's dancelike postures? Possibly it was the gradual evolution of person into myth. If such an individual ever existed, people continued creating Kokopelli images for many centuries after his death. Naturally, they would have invested their own experiences and expectations in these images.

Kokopölmana katsina doll by Hopi artist Jimmie Kewanwytewa, 1944.

Whatever the flute player's origins, a connection with fertility is a likely guess, for obvious reasons. But we are actually richer for not knowing for certain. If we could definitively parse the enigma of Kokopelli, he wouldn't be nearly so intriguing, would he?

HUNTING FOR KOKOPELLI

Stumbling onto an unexpected petroglyph or pictograph is like finding a secret spring in the desert: you can't take it home with you, but the knowledge is prize enough.

Rock art enthusiasts teach themselves to scan canyon walls and boulder piles with "petroglyph eyes," like a flycaster reads the rippling architecture of a stream. Binoculars are essential, and a sun low in the sky lights petroglyphs best from the side. In canyon country, petroglyphs, especially pictographs, are most likely to congregate on rocks protected from weather by an overhang. In the desert, hillsides of volcanic basalt rocks are always worth investigating. Water sources tended to attract rock artists—but the water table has plunged throughout the Southwest, so many of the springs and streams of A.D. 1200 are literally ancient history today.

In general, writes archaeologist Polly Schaafsma, the presence of rock art "correlates with places of power or cultural significance." Discovering it *in situ* can tell us something about the nature of a place—perhaps on a mystical or spiritual level that those of us who are not Native Americans normally are not aware of.

Tragically, rock art sites everywhere are under assault. Vandals have polluted them with mindless graffiti, and thieves have even chiseled glyphs off the rocks to take home. Because of this, park and forest rangers have become wary of giving directions to just anybody, but will often do so if convinced of honest intentions.

This should go without saying, but: Never touch rock art; body oil can degrade the image. If you find a potsherd or lithic—a stone tool or projectile point—leave it. The U.S. Archaeological Resources Protection Act of 1979 prohibits removing or defacing artifacts on federal land; most states have similar laws regarding state lands.

Apart from the law, context in archaeology is invaluable. An artifact on someone's private mantle has been muted forever. A flute player on a canyon wall continues a dialogue across the centuries.

Handprints and flute player in Canyon de Chelly (northeastern Arizona).
Modern Pueblo Indians view the handprint as a kind of signature.

KOKOPELLIANA

The American West—fierce, colossal, strange, contradictory, even mystical—has always resisted being grasped and understood in all its vastness. The reality of its history, culture, and landscape is overwhelming.

Former Arizona governor and U.S. Secretary of the Interior Bruce Babbitt tells a revealing story about a Grand Canyon sunset some years ago. As Babbitt watched, a tourist snapped a Polaroid of the spectacle unfolding in the sky. A small huddle then formed around the photographer to watch the image develop on a four-inch square of film, the people turning their backs on the inflamed heavens. The reality was too awesome to comprehend.

From the late-nineteenth century into the mid-twentieth, the West's most durable symbol was the rugged and dauntless cowboy, a heroic figure whose wealth resided in his independence. Many other symbols followed. The Mission Revival and Spanish Colonial Revival styles of architecture offered avenues for Anglos to buy into the myth of kindly priests and noble dons gently rolling civilization's carpet northward through Texas, New Mexico, Arizona, and California. Native American tribes made moves to capitalize on their

own cultures—Hopi ceramics and Navajo weaving were revived and adapted to the tourist market. Hopi artisans today gladly fashion Kokopelli pendants and earrings. Native artists such as the Navajo painter R. C. Gorman created romanticized images of their people—always noble and stoic in Gorman's depictions. It's harder to find art realistically interpreting contemporary life on the reservations.

In the 1980s, the coyote emerged as the West's preeminent emblem, adorning everything from switch plates to kitchen hot pads. Coyote seemed like an ideal representative for the West's core values: independent, adaptable, a survivor, bearing an air of casual superiority. The real-life coyote adapts to strange and hostile environments more capably than any other four-legged animal—which is precisely what the two-legged pioneers in the West had to do.

Kokopelli eclipsed Coyote in the 1990s, and his long run and global spread suggest an underlying power that reaches deeper than the image of the canine. Southwest folklorist James S. "Big Jim"

Silver earrings by Hopi artist Bernard Dawahoya, 1973.

Griffith believes some people might be drawn to the image of the flute player because of his latent naughtiness. "The tumid member is not obvious in most commercial representations," he says, "but everyone knows it's there." A fertility symbol speaks to humans of every age and culture, particularly if it seems to have a playful side. Procreation, after all, is fun.

The seductive power of the flute is another phenomenon that arises in different cultures—witness the legend of the Pied Piper, and the panpipes in Mozart's mystical opera *The Magic Flute*. These legends have become a part of our collective cultural memory, so we unconsciously associate flute players with magical powers.

Intriguingly, the rise of Kokopelli as an icon parallels the re-emergence of Native American flute music, most conspicuously popularized by the Navajo-Ute flutist R. Carlos Nakai. There is now an International Native American Flute Association, which conducts workshops and brings Native American flute enthusiasts, many of them non-Indians, together. Kathleen Joyce-Grendahl, a classically trained flutist who heads the organization, said the appeal of the native flute "has a lot to do with the nature of our society today—the chaos, the crazy schedules, the general complexity of

Pictographs (rock paintings) are more common than petroglyphs in Canyon de Chelly, where natural overhangs shelter them from weather.

life. People say that when they listen to the Native American flute, it provides them with a sense of peace, comfort, and calmness."

Just as significant is our urge to "own" a piece of an exotic culture—particularly one shrouded in so much mystery. The Anasazi culture presents many more questions than we have answers, most troublingly about the terrible thirteenth century. That was the age of the cliff dwellings, many of them apparently defensive, and probably clan-against-clan fighting for survival in the face of overpopulation and vanishing natural resources such as small game and firewood. It is a compelling story, and one that resonates in the booming Southwest of the twenty-first century, but all we can do is guess at the details. Kokopelli, bringing music and dance and apparently ready for a good time, seems to transcend the troubles. He is an affirmation: life goes on.

In an essay on the Kokopelli craze in *Archaeology* magazine, New Mexico writer John Neary almost nails it:

Well, maybe he is magic, maybe he and the other powerful symbols we call petroglyphs do contain some mystical ancient force. Maybe the hands of the artists who carved

A surprising number of Canyon de Chelly rock art sites exhibit twinned flute players.

him and his fellow rock figures were moved by some ele-
mental command that stirs us, too. Touching something
deep inside themselves, they thus managed to pull off the old

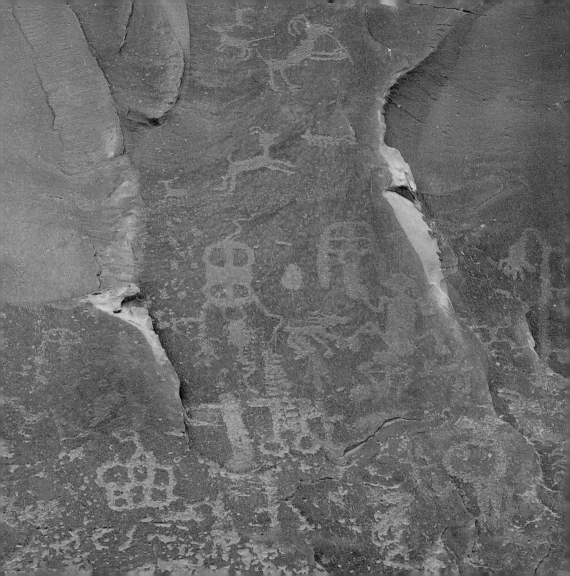

abracadabra that is every artist's dream: to reach across time to touch us, too, with their bold, stark, mysterious talismans, poetry in stone that speaks in a language we didn't even know we understood.

Forget the issue of mistaken identity; Kokopelli endures as a globally understandable symbol for joy, assuaging a profound longing in the human heart. He isn't so much mystical as he is universally emotional. The musician plays and dances and seduces, or so we imagine, against all the odds of deprivation, pain, and a crippling disease. We may trivialize the flute player by stamping him on our potholders and earrings, but perhaps we also learn from him.

The chances are excellent that we have reinvented, over-simplified, and/or misinterpreted Kokopelli—how could we expect to do otherwise, given his origins and long migrations through ancient cultures that left no written histories? But as the Western historian Richard White has written, "as people accept and assimilate myth, they act on the myths, and the myths become the basis for actions that shape history." We could do worse than shape our history with the inspiration of the flute player's cheerful serenade.

Zoomorphic flute players might be spirits or shamans assuming the form of animals (Sand Island Recreational Area, Utah).

‖ KOKOPELLI TALES ‖

Of course Kokopelli the modern icon does not appear in the traditional Native American stories of the Southwest. But hunchbacked and flute-playing figures certainly do, as well as mischief-makers, fabulous insects, and womanizers. Here, retold for modern readers, are three Southwestern folk tales that open windows into the cultures that also produced the fascinating little stick figure we know from ancient art.

COYOTE AND THE FLUTE PLAYER

This story from Zuni Pueblo may reveal aspects of Kokopelli the flute player, Kokopelli the trickster, and Kokopelli the insect. It is based on a tale collected and translated by Frank Hamilton Cushing and first published in his *Zuñi Folk Tales* (1901).

One fine, hot summer day long ago, Coyote went out hunting. As he wandered along he heard the sound of a flute and a voice that sang this song:

The final figure in a procession of anthropomorphs bears a flute player over his head (near Wupatki National Monument, Arizona).

> Cicada, cicada, playing a flute,
>
> High up in a pine tree, clinging, singing,
>
> And playing a flute, toot-toot,
>
> And playing a flute!

"Delightful!" cried Coyote, looking up. There, perched in a pine tree just above Coyote's head, sat Cicada, making music. "How well you play your flute!" Coyote gushed. He squatted down on his haunches, pricked up his ears, and grinned. But Coyote was polite only when he wanted something, and maybe not even then.

"Do you think so?" asked Cicada.

"Oh, yes!" said Coyote, moving closer. "Please teach me your song! I want to take it home and sing it to my children."

So Cicada sang again.

> Cicada, cicada, playing a flute,
>
> High up in a pine tree, clinging, singing,
>
> And playing a flute, toot-toot,
>
> And playing a flute!

"Now I'll try it," said Coyote, and he howled the song in a hoarse voice, making lots of mistakes. "Ha!" he laughed at the end. "I've got it, haven't I?"

Flute players are often found near figures with exaggerated hands and feet (Chinle Wash, San Juan River, Utah).

"Hmm," said Cicada. "Yes, more or less."

With a whisk of his tail Coyote set out for home, repeating the song to himself as he trotted along so he would not forget it. But he forgot to look where he was going, and suddenly he fell head over heels into Gopher's hole.

"Idiot Gopher!" Coyote snarled. "You fat pest! It's lucky for you that you're not home. You made me forget my song. Well, I'll just go back and get old Cicada to sing it again."

Sure enough, he found Cicada still sitting in the tree and singing.

"Very well," said Cicada, when he heard Coyote's tale. "But this time, please be more careful." And Cicada sang the song again.

> Cicada, cicada, playing a flute,
> High up in a pine tree, clinging, singing,
> And playing a flute, toot-toot,
> And playing a flute!

"Good! I've got it now!" said Coyote, and off he ran. "The children will love it," he said to himself. "They'll stop shrieking and fighting and listen to me quietly. Let's see—how does it go? Oh, yes! 'Cicada, cicada, playing a flute—'"

Some form of headdress embellishes many flute players (Canyon del Muerto, Arizona).

"Pff-ll-ttt! Squeee! Piu-piu!"

A flock of plump gray doves flapped out of the bushes right in front of Coyote's pointed nose, and they startled him so badly that he called them some terrible names.

"Piu-piu to you, too!" retorted the doves.

And then Coyote forgot his song. All he could remember was "Toot-toot."

Now, Cicada had suspected this might happen. And he also had his suspicions about Coyote, for he had heard evil rumors that Coyote sometimes snacked on insects, including cicadas. So Cicada decided to teach Coyote a lesson.

Poo-oof! First, Cicada swelled himself up inside his crisp golden shell. Then—crack!—he popped right out of it. Leaving his old skin behind, he crawled down the tree and found a clear quartz pebble on the ground. He carried the quartz up the tree and carefully placed it inside his empty skin, gluing the shell together again with pine pitch, and left the dummy Cicada perched in the tree. Then the real Cicada flew away to safety.

And just in the nick of time, for at that very moment who should appear but Coyote?

Roadside craft vendor's sign (Monument Valley, Utah).

"Blithering birdbrains!" he puffed. "I'm exhausted! Sing that song again, Cicada, and make it snappy!"

He waited. But Cicada did not answer.

"Hey! What's the matter? Are you deaf?" Coyote came up very close and squinted through the branches at the small figure in the pine tree. "Listen, you pipsqueak! I've lost my song again. Sing it one more time!"

No answer.

Now Coyote was getting angry. "Are you going to sing for me or not?" he demanded.

Silence.

"Look here!" shouted Coyote. He raised his pointed muzzle and wrinkled up his furry lips. "Do you see my teeth? This is your last chance. I'll give you till the count of four: One! Will you sing to me? Two! Don't be a stupid bug. Sing to me! Three! Better start singing NOW, or I'll eat you up and you'll never sing again! Four—!"

But not a peep, not a hum, not a single toot came out of Cicada.

"You filthy flute-playing tree-hugging maggot!" yelled Coyote. Unable to control himself any longer, he leaped into the air and snapped the Cicada shell right out of the pine tree. And then he bit it

Sinagua flute player (near Sedona, Arizona).

so hard that the quartz pebble broke his teeth, crushing the middle ones into little stumps and forcing the front teeth out into long fangs.

And that's why all Coyotes from that day to this have needle-sharp fangs in front and little short teeth behind. And Cicadas still leave hollow Cicada-shaped decoys behind them. And on hot summer days, you can still hear their music.

> Cicada, cicada, playing a flute,
> High up in a pine tree, clinging, singing,
> And playing a flute, toot-toot,
> And playing a flute!

BEAUTY AND THE BUG

Cochiti Pueblo in northern New Mexico is the setting for this story of insect love, reminiscent of the Greek myth of Cupid and Psyche. It is based on a tale collected by Ruth Benedict in the early 1920s and published in Bureau of American Ethnology Bulletin No. 98 (1932).

There was once a Cochiti *cacique,* or chief, whose daughter was very beautiful but very standoffish. She did not want to marry anyone.

Sinagua flute player (Honanki Ruin, near Sedona, Arizona).

Day after day, the lovelorn young men of Cochiti offered her exquisite marriage clothes—woven belts, white leather moccasins, and fine robes, or *mantas*—but she rejected them all. Night after night, her suitors put their heads together and plotted new ways to win her, but nothing worked. She refused them all, one after another.

Finally as a prank the young men went to a certain homely, bald-headed, burrowing bug named Biliiwai'ya (or Cicada).

"It's your turn," they said. "All the rest of us have failed. You must ask the beauty to marry *you*."

"What's the use?" said Biliiwai'ya. "You're much handsomer than I am. Why, I'm an insect! And besides, I'm bald."

"Try it anyway!" they said, egging him on.

So Biliiwai'ya made himself a glossy black wig, cutting thick bangs across the forehead just as the men from Cochiti do. The other young men laughed at the sight, but really once that wig was on his head, the cicada looked like a handsome boy. And in spite of all their laughter he went to the girl's house to ask her to marry him.

To everyone's amazement, she stood up and smiled when she saw him, for she liked this new boy and thought he was very attractive. And she did marry him.

Sheep depicted in several different "styles" surround this Canyon del Muerto flute player.

At first all went well—very well indeed—and they were extremely happy. Every night, when his beautiful wife was sound asleep, Biliiwai'ya took off his wig. But then one night she woke up and looked over at her sleeping husband.

"What have I done?" she thought, absolutely horrified.

The black wig lay by his side, and her husband was bald—and he was a cicada!

"Help, help, I'm in bed with a hideous bug!" she screamed. She leaped out of bed and scrambled up the ladder to escape.

But then Biliiwai'ya woke, clapped on his wig, and flew after her.

Love conquers all. The cicada and the beauty became the parents of six children, all bald, but Biliiwai'ya made a beautiful wig for each one.

MAN CRAZY

A hunchbacked husband and a frustrated wife are the main characters in this tale, which comes from several Hopi sources, including Ekkehart Malotki's *Kokopelli: The Making of an Icon* (2000).

Once, in a faraway village on top of a mesa in Hopiland, there was a young man who had no family. Because he was an orphan, he grew

up very ignorant of many common things—he didn't know how to dance, or weave, or hunt anything bigger than a cottontail rabbit, or grow corn. This young man didn't even have a grandmother, and grandmothers teach a person a lot. So he was a loner, and he was especially ignorant about girls.

But it so happened that a young woman fell in love with him, and when he married her, he began to learn many things. Since he didn't know how to weave, he couldn't make her wedding clothes, which was the traditional duty of a Hopi bridegroom. So he decided to learn to weave, and he carded wool and spun it and wove it far into the night, and he never came to bed with his wife.

First she lay in bed and waited. Then she fell asleep alone, and then when she woke up she was unhappy. But her husband just went on weaving and weaving, and his wife grew angry. She began to treat him badly, and he started to sulk, and then she turned man-crazy and ran around the village with any man or boy she could find. It was a scandal!

The miserable young man wandered away to the edge of the mesa where the village stood, and he sat there on the brink of the cliff, wondering what to do.

"If I jump off, I'll never have to go home again," he said to him-self. "And she'll never make me suffer any more. *She* won't care if I'm dead, and I have no relatives to care, either."

As the sun went down, he leaped off the precipice. He fell a long way down before he hit the ground and lost consciousness, but he did not die. The next thing he knew, a voice was talking in his ear, and the young man opened his eyes and saw Badger, who lived in a den at the foot of the mesa.

"How could you do this to yourself?" asked Badger. "It's foolish, very foolish! I know all about your problem, and jumping off a cliff won't cure it. You should have asked for help instead. What you need is medicine, my boy. You need stiffening medicine, and I have it!"

"Give it to me, please," groaned the man, who was in great pain. "I think I broke my back."

"It won't help your back," said Badger. "Oh, no! It's no good for that! It works somewhere else, my friend. Your back will just have to get well by itself, but you won't die. You'll get better. Come on, you'll see."

Although the young man was terribly injured, he managed to crawl into Badger's den, where he lived until he got well. Meanwhile

A "stick figure" flute player in east-central Arizona is fully outfitted with headdress, hump, and phallus.

Kachina World, watercolor painting by Hopi
artist Michael Kabotie, circa early 1960s.

up on top of the mesa, his man-crazy wife didn't even bother to look for him. She was so busy with all the other men in the village that she never missed her husband.

When the young man healed, he was hunchbacked.

"Never mind!" said Badger. "Here, take the stiffening medicine and go home."

So the hunchbacked man slowly climbed the trail to the top of the mesa where the village stood. It was springtime, and he gathered flowers as he went. When he reached the village with his arms full of flowers, he sang a song:

> It's spring.
> Here I come,
> Bringing flowers,
> Seeds and flowers.
> Who wants flowers?

Contemporary painting on stone by Navajo artist Nathaniel Gorman of Chinle, Arizona.

Badger's medicine was very powerful. In spite of the young man's hump, all the girls and women came out of their houses and followed him home. And there stood his wife. She was overjoyed to see him, hump and all, and she stretched out her arms, which he filled with flowers.

As time passed, and spring came again and again, many children were born to them. So it happened that the lonely orphan fathered a large family, but he learned to be a good hunter and farmer, and he fed them.

SUGGESTED READING

Malotki, Ekkehart. *Kokopelli: The Making of an Icon.* Lincoln, Nebraska: Bison Books, 2004.

Schaafsma, Polly. *Indian Rock Art of the Southwest.* Albuquerque, New Mexico:
University of New Mexico Press, 1986.

Slifer, Dennis, and James Duffield. *Kokopelli: Fluteplayer Images in Rock Art.* Santa Fe,
New Mexico: Ancient City Press, 1994.

Stuart, David E. *Anasazi America.* Albuquerque, New Mexico:
University of New Mexico Press, 2000.

Thybony, Scott. *Rock Art of the American Southwest.* Portland,
Oregon: Scott Graphic Arts Center Publishing, 1994.

PHOTOGRAPHY © AS FOLLOWS:

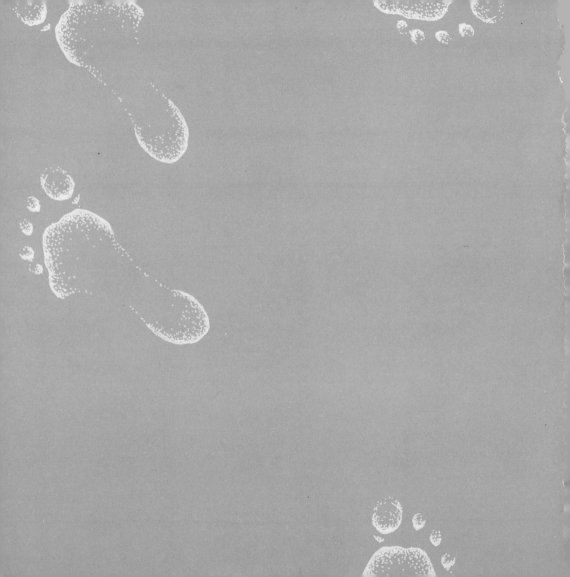

RIO NUEVO PUBLISHERS®
P.O. Box 5250, Tucson, Arizona 85703-0250
(520) 623-9558, www.rionuevo.com

Design: Karen Schober, Seattle, Washington

Library of Congress Cataloging-in-Publication Data

Cheek, Larry.
  Kokopelli / Lawrence W. Cheek.
     p. cm. -- (Look West series)
  Includes bibliographical references.
  ISBN 1-887896-63-5 (cloth)
 1. Kokopelli (Pueblo deity) 2. Pueblo mythology. 3. Pueblo art. 4. Pueblo Indians--Antiquities. 5.
Rock paintings--Southwest, New. 6. Petroglyphs--Southwest, New. 7. Southwest, New--Antiquities.
I. Title. II. Series: Look West.
  E99.P9C476 2005
  299.7'84--dc22

                        2004016431

Printed in Hong Kong
10 9 8 7 6 5 4 3 2 1

KOKOPELLI

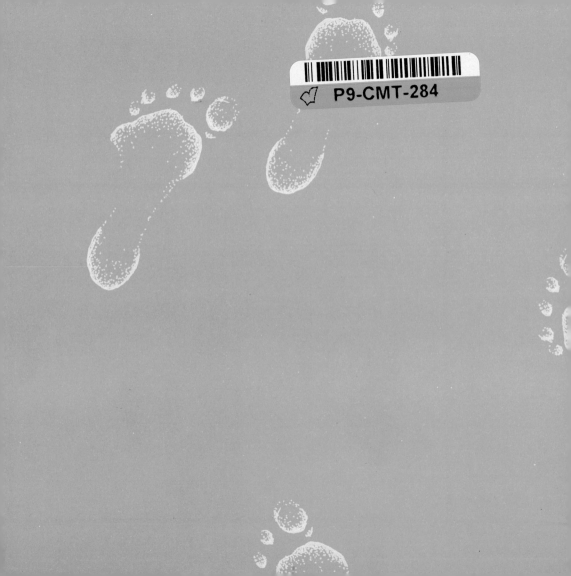

P9-CMT-284